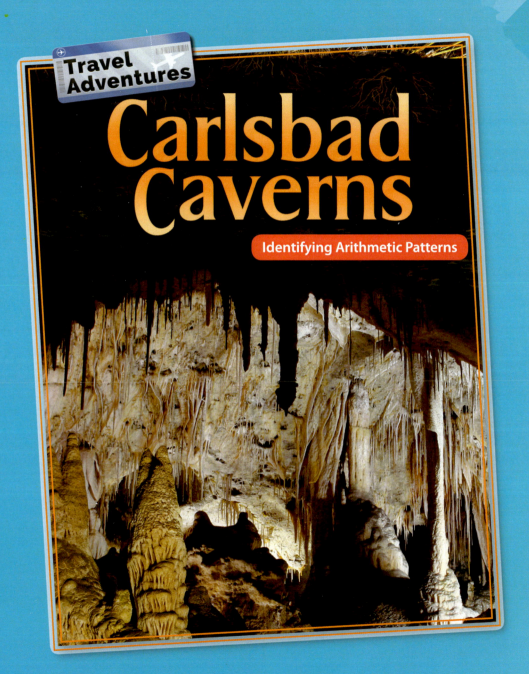

Travel Adventures

Carlsbad Caverns

Identifying Arithmetic Patterns

Dona Herweck Rice

Consultants

Michele Ogden, Ed.D
Principal, Irvine Unified School District

Jennifer Robertson, M.A.Ed.
Teacher, Huntington Beach City School District

Publishing Credits
Rachelle Cracchiolo, M.S.Ed., *Publisher*
Conni Medina, M.A.Ed., *Managing Editor*
Dona Herweck Rice, *Series Developer*
Emily R. Smith, M.A.Ed., *Series Developer*
Diana Kenney, M.A.Ed., NBCT, *Content Director*
Stacy Monsman, M.A., *Editor*
Kevin Panter, *Graphic Designer*

Image Credits: p. 8 GIPhotoStock/Science Source; p. 14 Michael Nichols/Getty Images; pp. 14-15 John Cancalosi/Getty Images; p. 15 Rick & Nora Bowers/Alamy Stock Photo; pp. 16-17 NPS Photo/Peter Jones; p. 18 (top) Michael Runkel New Mexico/Alamy Stock Photo; pp. 20-21 Susan E. Degginger/Alamy Stock Photo; pp. 22-23 Doug Meek/Getty Images; p. 23 Brendan Smialowski/AFP/Getty Images; p. 24 Jim West/Alamy Stock Photo; p. 25 RGB Ventures/SuperStock/Alamy Stock Photo; p. 26 Chris Howes/Wild Places Photography/Alamy Stock Photo; back cover Rick & Nora Bowers/Alamy Stock Photo; all other images from iStock and/or Shutterstock.

Library of Congress Cataloging-in-Publication Data
Names: Rice, Dona.
Title: Travel adventures : Carlsbad Caverns / Dona Herweck Rice.
Other titles: Carlsbad Caverns
Description: Huntington Beach, CA : Teacher Created Materials, [2017] | Audience: K to grade 3. | Includes index.
Identifiers: LCCN 2016053310 (print) | LCCN 2017007838 (ebook) | ISBN 9781480757981 (pbk.) | ISBN 9781480758629 (eBook)
Subjects: LCSH: Carlsbad Caverns (N.M.)--Juvenile literature. | Carlsbad Caverns National Park (N.M.)--Juvenile literature.
Classification: LCC F802.C28 R53 2017 (print) | LCC F802.C28 (ebook) | DDC 978.9/42--dc23
LC record available at https://lccn.loc.gov/2016053310

Teacher Created Materials
5301 Oceanus Drive
Huntington Beach, CA 92649-1030
http://www.tcmpub.com

ISBN 978-1-4807-5798-1
© 2018 Teacher Created Materials, Inc.

Table of Contents

Stepping into the Earth 4

Years in the Making 6

Spelunking through the Caverns 14

Modern Conveniences 22

Preserving the Caverns 27

Problem Solving 28

Glossary 30

Index 31

Answer Key 32

Stepping into the Earth

You step carefully down a winding cement pathway. The path drops down, down, down below the level of the land. The air gets cooler with every step. The light gets dimmer, too, as you leave the sun behind. Birds dart overhead and race down the path ahead of you.

The path leads into a tall, wide opening. It looks like the earth is yawning. This is the mouth of the caverns. You are getting ready to step into the earth itself! The air is damp, and it smells strongly of bat **guano**, or poop. The floor of the cave is covered in it!

You have just stepped through the entrance to Carlsbad Caverns. The caverns are a U.S. National Park. People want to **preserve** this unique spot for years to come.

LET'S EXPLORE MATH

One property of addition is that two odd numbers always have an even sum. Two even numbers also have an even sum. But, an odd number and an even number have an odd sum. These are constant patterns in arithmetic.

Now, imagine you take 335 steps into the cavern. Your brother, who has shorter legs, takes 383 steps. Will the sum of your steps be odd or even?

the winding pathway into the entrance of Carlsbad Caverns

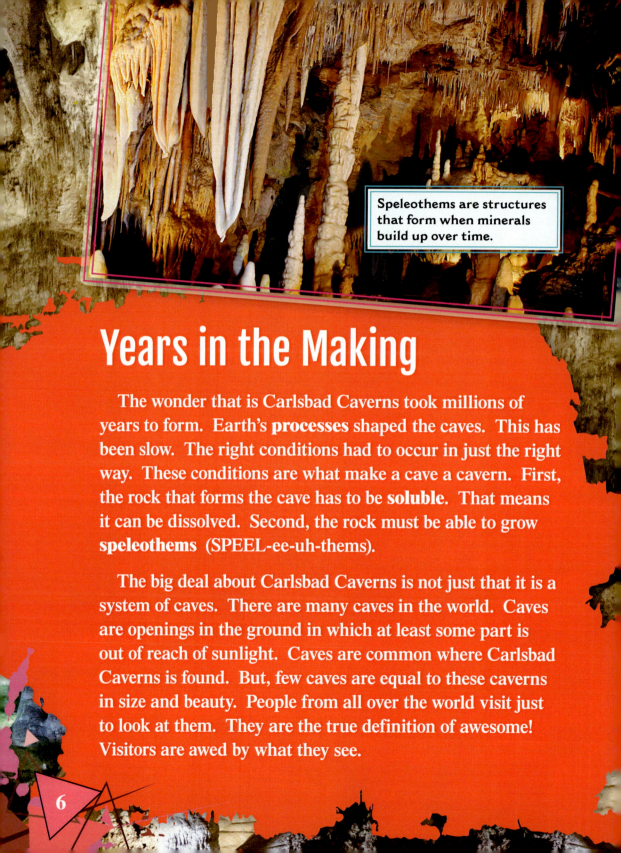

Speleothems are structures that form when minerals build up over time.

Years in the Making

The wonder that is Carlsbad Caverns took millions of years to form. Earth's **processes** shaped the caves. This has been slow. The right conditions had to occur in just the right way. These conditions are what make a cave a cavern. First, the rock that forms the cave has to be **soluble**. That means it can be dissolved. Second, the rock must be able to grow **speleothems** (SPEEL-ee-uh-thems).

The big deal about Carlsbad Caverns is not just that it is a system of caves. There are many caves in the world. Caves are openings in the ground in which at least some part is out of reach of sunlight. Caves are common where Carlsbad Caverns is found. But, few caves are equal to these caverns in size and beauty. People from all over the world visit just to look at them. They are the true definition of awesome! Visitors are awed by what they see.

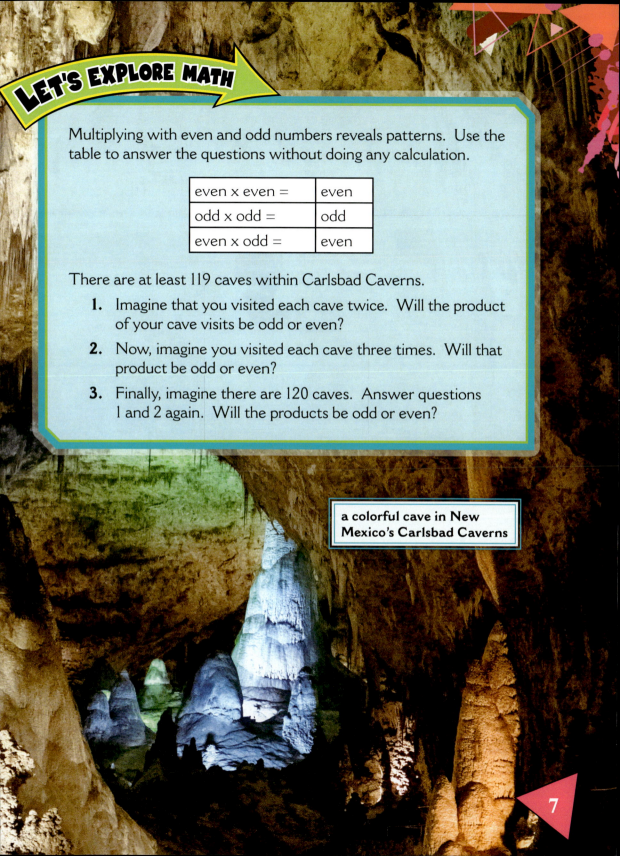

LET'S EXPLORE MATH

Multiplying with even and odd numbers reveals patterns. Use the table to answer the questions without doing any calculation.

even x even =	even
odd x odd =	odd
even x odd =	even

There are at least 119 caves within Carlsbad Caverns.

1. Imagine that you visited each cave twice. Will the product of your cave visits be odd or even?

2. Now, imagine you visited each cave three times. Will that product be odd or even?

3. Finally, imagine there are 120 caves. Answer questions 1 and 2 again. Will the products be odd or even?

a colorful cave in New Mexico's Carlsbad Caverns

A piece of limestone corrodes in acid.

the edge of a waterpool in Carlsbad Caverns

Corrosion at Work

There are many ways for caves to form. For example, tubes of lava may form caves of many shapes and sizes. Caves may also form through the movement of Earth's **plates**. But, caverns like those at Carlsbad form when rock is dissolved. This happens through **corrosion**. **Acids** in water seep through cracks in rock. Over time, they wear away the rock. The openings they carve out grow deeper and wider. The caverns spread below Earth's surface. They look like the sprawling burrows dug by giant field mice!

Let's be clear. Water itself is not an acid. But rainwater may collect acid from Earth's atmosphere. When it does, the acid in water carves out the caverns. And it does a whole lot more as well!

Drip, Drip, Drip

While they were being formed, the movement of Earth's plates lifted the caves. Acidic water drained away to reveal huge rooms and pathways. But there was more work to be done before the caverns would become what we know them as today. In fact, that work is still going on!

This is what happens. Fresh water **percolates** into the caverns. It comes from rain and water stored in the ground. The water drips steadily through the rock. This is why the caverns stay damp and musty. The water collects minerals and gas as it drips. The gas changes and becomes **carbonic acid**. The minerals and acid in the water get to work. They build the beautiful formations visitors flock to see. They do it drip by drip.

Limestone formations like these develop over many years.

Water still shapes cave formations.

LET'S EXPLORE MATH

One property of addition tells us that adding 0 to any number will result in the same number. The zero property of multiplication tells us that any number multiplied by 0 is 0. So, adding 0 to any number results in the number, but multiplying any number by 0 results in 0. These are constant patterns.

At Carlsbad Caverns, you and your brother decide to stand very still and listen for drips. Using these properties, answer the following questions. Think about the pattern.

1. You hear 9 drips. Your brother isn't paying attention and hears 0. How many are heard in total?

2. Your brother hears 8 drips. You get distracted and hear 0. How many are heard in total?

3. You hear 6 drips. Your brother hears 6 drips. Then, someone yells and you both hear 0 drips. How many drips are heard in total?

4. Using the numbers in problem 3, what happens when you multiply instead of add? Use the property.

11

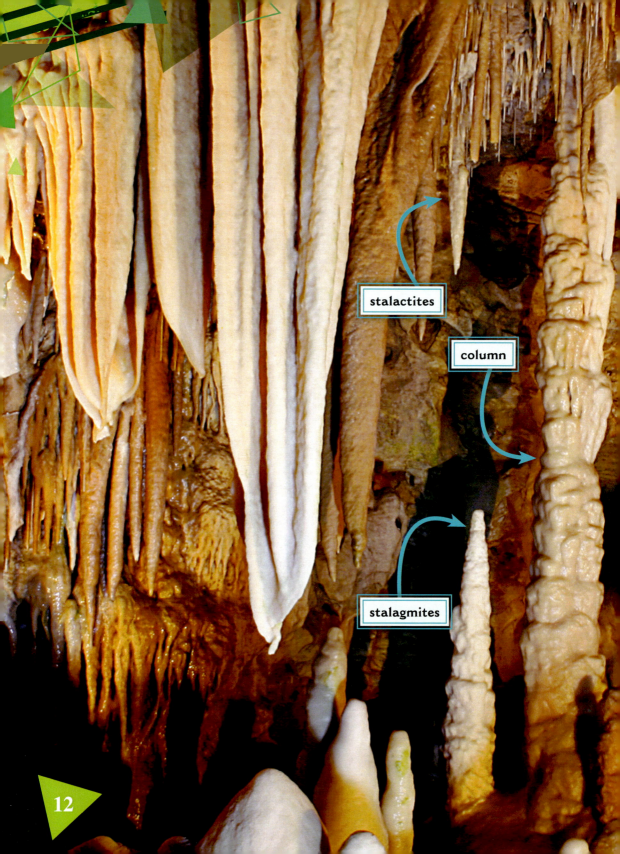

soda straws

popcorn

These beautiful formations are speleothems. They seem to grow from the cavern walls. It is stunning to think they formed just one drip at a time.

Most of the speleothems are **stalactites** (stuh-LACK-tites). They form when minerals bond to the ceiling. Others are **stalagmites** (stuh-LAG-mites). They form when minerals build up from the ground. Minerals may also form columns. Or they may form popcorn or soda straws. These are all types of speleothems.

Carbonic acid plays a role. The dripping water **deposits** minerals that were dissolved by the acid. They become solid again. They may become part of a soda straw. They may become popcorn. Or, they may simply drip away.

No matter how, structures are being formed all the time in the caverns. Changes may come slowly. But the caverns are changing all the time.

Spelunking through the Caverns

Spelunkers are enthusiastic about Carlsbad Caverns. That is the name for people who like to explore caves. In the caverns, they get to see the unusual formations that make these so much more than typical caves.

A spelunker examines formations deep within Carlsbad Caverns.

Going Batty!

After you pass through the winding entrance to the caverns, you may stop to take a breath. You've just traveled 200 feet (61 meters) below the surface! It is dark, and the air is cool. To your left is a giant cave. It's called the Bat Cave. But no, Batman® doesn't live there. More bats than you can imagine do! They sleep during the day. At dusk, they fly out of the cavern entrance. They swarm the sky in a giant mass. It is breathtaking to see! If you visit during the spring or summer, you might get a chance to see them soar.

LET'S EXPLORE MATH

Although often sleeping, the bats at Carlsbad Caverns are all around you and can be all but impossible to count!

A property of addition and multiplication states that even when you change the order of addends or factors, you still get the same sum or product. For example, $3 + 2 = 5$ and $2 + 3 = 5$. Also, $3 \times 2 = 6$ and $2 \times 3 = 6$. This is a pattern you can count on!

Keep this property in mind as you answer these questions:

1. You count 6 groups of 3 bats each. How many bats are there?

2. If you count 3 groups of 6 bats each, how many bats do you have then?

3. How is the property shown in questions 1 and 2?

Main Corridor

The next part of your journey is along the Main Corridor. It is a long path with high ceilings. There is plenty of room to look around. You soon pass Devil's Spring and Devil's Den. These names tell you something about how early explorers felt in the caverns! At Devil's Den, you are about 500 ft. (152 m) below the surface.

As you walk down the steep path, you come to Witch's Finger. It stands alone and points up from the ground. It looks very much like the long, bony finger the fairy-tale witch jabs at Hansel in *Hansel and Gretel*. But it is about five times as tall as a boy like Hansel would be.

Up next is Iceberg Rock. That's where the path turns. The "rock" once hung from above. But its weight dropped it to the floor. It weighs more than 200,000 tons!

Devil's Spring

a place to snack and shop deep within the caverns

18

Big Room

As you pass Iceberg Rock, the path twists and turns. It becomes narrow and then widens again. With a guide, you can travel down to King's Palace and Queen's Chamber. They sit more than 800 ft. (244 m) below the surface. But on your own, you will turn left to Big Room. Now, the show really begins!

First, you step onto Big Room's wide, flat area. People are milling about. Many of them have just stepped from an elevator. It shoots down hundreds of feet from the visitor's center on the surface.

Across the landing is something else made by humans. There's a snack bar! That's right. Deep in the caverns, you can grab a bite to eat. You can even pick up a souvenir.

the view of Big Room from the walkway

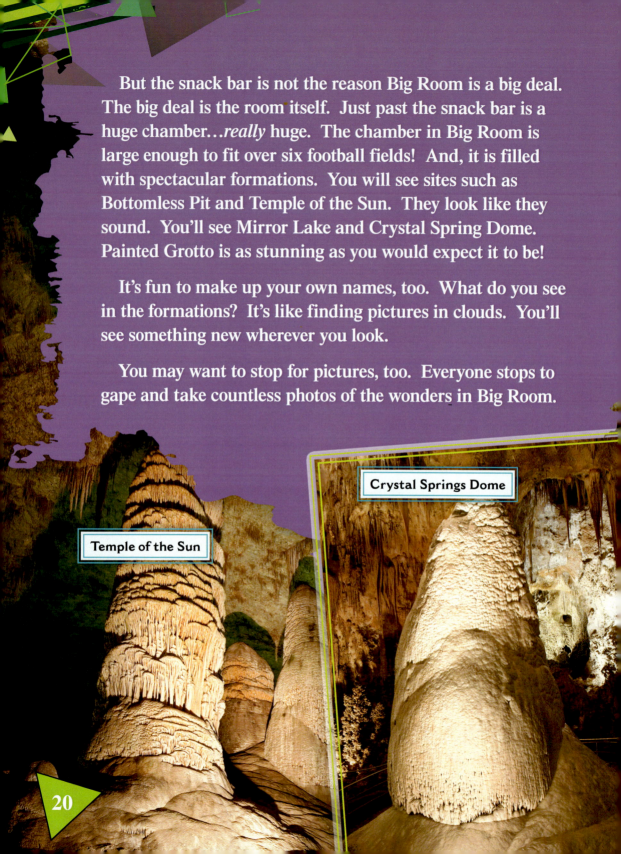

But the snack bar is not the reason Big Room is a big deal. The big deal is the room itself. Just past the snack bar is a huge chamber…*really* huge. The chamber in Big Room is large enough to fit over six football fields! And, it is filled with spectacular formations. You will see sites such as Bottomless Pit and Temple of the Sun. They look like they sound. You'll see Mirror Lake and Crystal Spring Dome. Painted Grotto is as stunning as you would expect it to be!

It's fun to make up your own names, too. What do you see in the formations? It's like finding pictures in clouds. You'll see something new wherever you look.

You may want to stop for pictures, too. Everyone stops to gape and take countless photos of the wonders in Big Room.

Temple of the Sun

Crystal Springs Dome

LET'S EXPLORE MATH

Carlsbad Caverns is filled with patterns of formations. The patterns create beautiful things to see. Math patterns can be beautiful, too! Take a look at this addition table. The addends appear across the top row and down the left column. The sums are where they intersect. Study the table. Then, answer these questions. Look for the patterns!

1. What do you notice when the sum is 5?
2. What do you notice when the sum is 0?
3. What do you notice when the sum is 10?
4. What do you notice about patterns among all the sums?

+	0	1	2	3	4	5	6	7	8	9	10
0	0	1	2	3	4	5	6	7	8	9	10
1	1	2	3	4	5	6	7	8	9	10	11
2	2	3	4	5	6	7	8	9	10	11	12
3	3	4	5	6	7	8	9	10	11	12	13
4	4	5	6	7	8	9	10	11	12	13	14
5	5	6	7	8	9	10	11	12	13	14	15
6	6	7	8	9	10	11	12	13	14	15	16
7	7	8	9	10	11	12	13	14	15	16	17
8	8	9	10	11	12	13	14	15	16	17	18
9	9	10	11	12	13	14	15	16	17	18	19
10	10	11	12	13	14	15	16	17	18	19	20

Painted Grotto

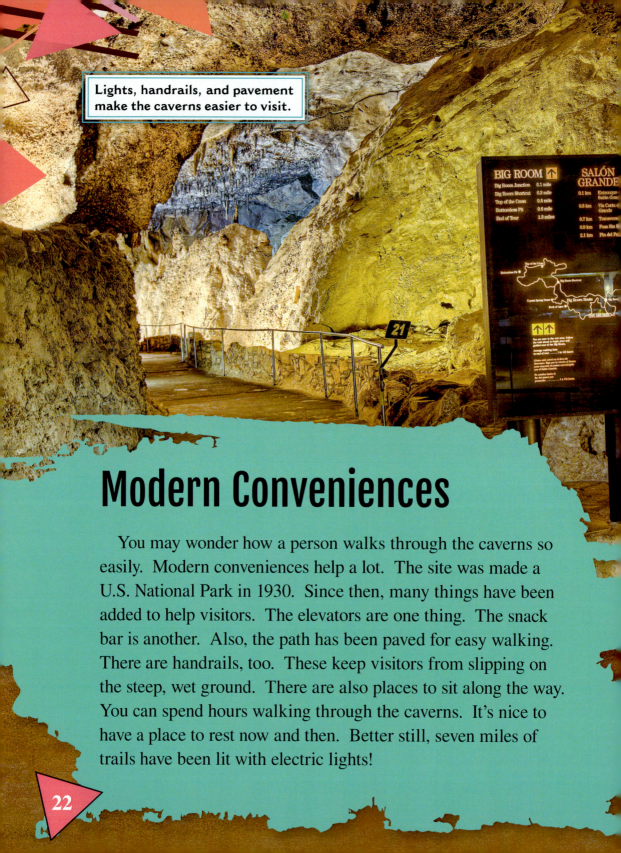

Lights, handrails, and pavement make the caverns easier to visit.

Modern Conveniences

You may wonder how a person walks through the caverns so easily. Modern conveniences help a lot. The site was made a U.S. National Park in 1930. Since then, many things have been added to help visitors. The elevators are one thing. The snack bar is another. Also, the path has been paved for easy walking. There are handrails, too. These keep visitors from slipping on the steep, wet ground. There are also places to sit along the way. You can spend hours walking through the caverns. It's nice to have a place to rest now and then. Better still, seven miles of trails have been lit with electric lights!

President Obama and his family tour Carlsbad Caverns.

23

Just Like the Old Days

But the whole park doesn't have these modern conveniences! Slaughter Canyon Cave is kept in its natural state. You can only explore it with a park ranger. There are no paved paths. There are no electric lights. Visitors must bring flashlights. It is a half-mile (0.8-kilometer) hike just to reach the cave entrance. The tour is another two to three hours of walking. But visitors say it's worth the time and effort.

A special highlight of the tour is called Christmas Tree. It is not a tree at all. It is a speleothem column. The column is covered in crystals. They sparkle in the light of flashlights.

Visitors can also tour old bat guano mines. The guano is thick on the cave floor. It was once mined for farming.

People wait to enter Slaughter Canyon Cave.

Christmas Tree

LET'S EXPLORE MATH

One thing you do a lot of at Carlsbad Caverns is walk! Take a look at this multiplication table. The factors appear across the top row and down the left column. The products are where they intersect. Study the table. Then, answer these questions.

1. You and 5 other people (6 total) each take 4 steps. That is 24 steps in all. How many others ways can you and a different group of people reach 24 steps by taking the same number of steps each?

2. If every step you take is 2 feet long, will you ever step an odd number of feet?

×	1	2	3	4	5	6	7	8	9	10	11	12
1	1	2	3	4	5	6	7	8	9	10	11	12
2	2	4	6	8	10	12	14	16	18	20	22	24
3	3	6	9	12	15	18	21	24	27	30	33	36
4	4	8	12	16	20	24	28	32	36	40	44	48
5	5	10	15	20	25	30	35	40	45	50	55	60
6	6	12	18	24	30	36	42	48	54	60	66	72
7	7	14	21	28	35	42	49	56	63	70	77	84
8	8	16	24	32	40	48	56	64	72	80	88	96
9	9	18	27	36	45	54	63	72	81	90	99	108
10	10	20	30	40	50	60	70	80	90	100	110	120
11	11	22	33	44	55	66	77	88	99	110	121	132
12	12	24	36	48	60	72	84	96	108	120	132	144

25

Preserving the Caverns

Carlsbad Caverns was made a U.S. National Park to preserve it. It was once in danger. People can damage nature without even knowing it. Sometimes, just walking over an area can harm it.

There are rules at the caverns that visitors must follow. Stay on the paths. Do not sit on the speleothems. Do not write on or mark them either. Rangers work at the caverns to teach people. They also help people follow the rules. And people pay to visit the caverns. The money helps pay for their care.

Some people are tempted to take a piece of the caverns home with them. Or they want to carve their names on rocks. But Carlsbad Caverns belongs to all of us. As the saying goes, we should take only pictures and memories. And we should leave only footprints.

Problem Solving

At Carlsbad Caverns, there are patterns of speleothems everywhere. Looking for patterns in formations is a lot like looking for patterns in arithmetic. Addition and multiplication properties are filled with patterns. They can help you understand math concepts.

Use the addition and multiplication tables on the right to answer the questions.

1. Looking at a room of stalactites, you see they are in groups of 5. When you look at multiples of 5 on the multiplication table, what do you notice?

2. There are stalagmites in groups of 3 in a chamber. When you look at the multiples of 3 on the multiplication table, what do you notice?

3. You count the stalagmites in one cavern. There are 13 groups of 13. Add factors of 13 to the multiplication table. Extend the pattern to show all the products leading to 13×13.

4. All the multiples of 2, 4, 6, 8, 10, and 12 are even. Is there ever a row or column of sums on the addition table that are all even? Why or why not?

5. Can you make any other comparisons between the addition and multiplication tables?

+	0	1	2	3	4	5	6	7	8	9	10
0	0	1	2	3	4	5	6	7	8	9	10
1	1	2	3	4	5	6	7	8	9	10	11
2	2	3	4	5	6	7	8	9	10	11	12
3	3	4	5	6	7	8	9	10	11	12	13
4	4	5	6	7	8	9	10	11	12	13	14
5	5	6	7	8	9	10	11	12	13	14	15
6	6	7	8	9	10	11	12	13	14	15	16
7	7	8	9	10	11	12	13	14	15	16	17
8	8	9	10	11	12	13	14	15	16	17	18
9	9	10	11	12	13	14	15	16	17	18	19
10	10	11	12	13	14	15	16	17	18	19	20

×	1	2	3	4	5	6	7	8	9	10	11	12
1	1	2	3	4	5	6	7	8	9	10	11	12
2	2	4	6	8	10	12	14	16	18	20	22	24
3	3	6	9	12	15	18	21	24	27	30	33	36
4	4	8	12	16	20	24	28	32	36	40	44	48
5	5	10	15	20	25	30	35	40	45	50	55	60
6	6	12	18	24	30	36	42	48	54	60	66	72
7	7	14	21	28	35	42	49	56	63	70	77	84
8	8	16	24	32	40	48	56	64	72	80	88	96
9	9	18	27	36	45	54	63	72	81	90	99	108
10	10	20	30	40	50	60	70	80	90	100	110	120
11	11	22	33	44	55	66	77	88	99	110	121	132
12	12	24	36	48	60	72	84	96	108	120	132	144

Glossary

acids—substances with a sour taste that can dissolve metals and other materials

carbonic acid—a type of acid that is based in carbon

corrosion—the breaking apart or dissolving of something

deposits—leaves an amount of something on a surface

guano—waste material from birds and bats

percolates—passes through slowly

plates—large, movable segments of Earth's lithosphere

preserve—protect and keep safe for the future

processes—natural events that result in gradual changes

soluble—able to be dissolved in a liquid

speleothems—formations created by the depositing of minerals, such as stalactites or stalagmites

spelunkers—people who study and explore caves

stalactites—speleothems that build downward from a ceiling

stalagmites—speleothems that extend upward from the ground

Index

acid, 8–10, 13

Bat Cave, 15

bats, 4 15

Big Room, 19–20

Bottomless Pit, 20

Christmas Tree, 24–25

column, 12–13, 24

corrosion, 9

Crystal Spring Dome, 20

Devil's Den, 17

Devil's Spring, 17

guano, 4, 24

Iceberg Rock, 17, 19

King's Palace, 19

Main Corridor, 17

Mirror Lake, 20

Painted Grotto, 20–21

popcorn, 13

Queen's Chamber, 19

Slaughter Canyon Cave, 24

soda straws, 13

speleothems, 6, 13, 27–28

spelunkers, 14

stalactites, 12–13, 28

stalagmites, 12–13, 28

Temple of the Sun, 20

U.S. National Park, 4, 22, 27

Witch's Finger, 16–17

31

Answer Key

Let's Explore Math

page 5:

even

page 7:

1. even
2. odd
3. even; even

page 11:

1. 9
2. 8
3. 12
4. 0

page 15:

1. 18
2. 18
3. Even though the order of factors changed, the product did not.

page 21:

1. Answers will vary but may include: each addend is 5 or less; sums of 5 are on a diagonal.
2. Only addends of 0 can equal 0.
3. Answers will vary but may include: 10 is the sum that appears the most on the table; sums of 10 are on a diagonal.
4. Answers will vary but may include: the same sums appear on a diagonal; sums increase to the right or down but decrease to the left or up.

page 25:

1. 5: 2 people × 12 steps; 3 people × 8 steps; 4 people × 6 steps; 8 people × 3 steps; 12 people × 2 steps
2. No

Problem Solving

1. The digit in the ones place is 5 or 0; the multiples alternate between odd and even.
2. Multiples alternate between odd and even; 3, 6, 9, and 12 have similar factors.
3. 13, 26, 39, 52, 65, 78, 91, 104, 117, 130, 143, 156, 169
4. No; when adding one more, sometimes two equal groups cannot be made, so the sum is odd.
5. Answers will vary but may include: The first columns of each table are the same.